Wri

Your

Adventure

A brief guide for adventure travellers

Duncan Gough

Matador
9 Priory Business Park,
Wistow Road, Kibworth Beauchamp,
Leicestershire. LE8 0RX
Tel: (+44) 116 279 2299
Fax: (+44) 116 279 2277
Email: books@troubador.co.uk
Web: www.troubador.co.uk/matador

ISBN 978 1788036 887

British Library Cataloguing in Publication Data.
A catalogue record for this book is available from the British Library.

Typeset in 13pt Segoe UI
Printed and bound by CPI Group (UK) Ltd, Croydon, CR0 4YY

Matador is an imprint of Troubador Publishing Ltd

CONTENTS

This book is written for the adventure traveller who wishes to keep a record of their journey whether for personal use, family and grandchildren or perhaps for a wider audience.

It is based on my own experience as a traveller who writes.

Introduction

However much of a record you make of your journey there are a few basics that are best thought about before you set off.

The first thing to think about is how you are going to record it. These days many people will automatically figure to use their smart phone, as they go along. This is certainly a valid possibility, but one which does have some drawbacks. How often do you need to charge it? Are you always going to be able to find somewhere to do so? How vulnerable is it to being dropped or getting wet? It can be a target for pickpockets. How easy is it to transfer to a computer upon your return? Is it going to be easy to structure the information as you record it? On the photographic side, will the pictures have a high enough resolution? 300 dpi is needed for professional printing (See page 32). Quality can also be an issue with sound and video.

Personally I believe in the good old-fashioned sketchbook/journal as the primary record. It is pretty rugged and is not likely to get nicked. It can be well supported by a smart phone or a tablet, camera and even a solid state or mini-disc recorder.

I see the record of a journey or adventure as a kind of layer cake. The number of layers you put down is your choice, but you always need the bottom layer, - the facts, the objective reality (see diagram opposite).

EDIT AND STRUCTURE

BEYOND THE WORD

FICTION

LANDSCAPE AND CHARACTER

HISTORY AND CULTURE

REFERENCING

IMAGINATION AS REALITY

MORE PERSONAL INVOLVEMENT

STRIKING A CHORD

BASIC PERSONAL IMPRESSIONS

FACTS

Facts

One way to record these is to make up a spreadsheet with the things you feel are going to be important. For example if one was walking the Camino de Santiago, one might want a column for people, fellow *peregrinos*, route details, food, accommodation, birds. Think about the things that will interest you as you travel. It is easy enough to make yourself a little booklet of sheets, or if you've

DATE	TIME	PLACE	WEATHER	EVENT

got an old filofax lying dusty in a corner, make use of that. Or set it out in your tablet or smart phone.

The important thing is to have a framework for collecting this basic information. The next and all important step is to use it, getting into a <u>habit</u> of making notes when you stop for lunch. Similarly taking a few minutes as a wind-down at the end of the day pays real dividends.

When it comes to routes, I favour carrying paper maps. In Spain I buy new ones every couple of years; firstly they get tatty and secondly new roads get built. I will mark on my intended day's route in one highlighter colour and then use another at the end of the day for the actual route taken. I do not like handing over control of my travel to an electronic 'GPS' brain, and even if you take care to find interesting places and plot them into your route you are then almost bound to follow it.

I like getting a bit lost, or seeing an interesting village name and turning off on a detour. In Spain a *garganta* is a throat or a gorge so, when riding the flanks of the Sierra de Gredos and seeing a road sign for Garganta de Olla, I took it. An *olla* by the way, is a pot. My detour was a good 20 km and well worth it. Stopping for some bread and chorizo for my lunch in the small town of Garganta, I asked the store owner about the *garganta*, he told me it was well worth visiting and gave me good directions. It was a lovely river valley with walks going up into the gorge from which the river tumbled and laughed across boulders and small falls. A dipper (a sort of underwater blackbird) flicked and flitted. By a grand pool for swimming in, the river stumbled down a rock shelf in which were a number of stone ground circular holes. I had found the pots.

Sometimes the weather takes a hand. Those giant, dark jellyfish storm clouds, with trailing stingers of rain are to the west, right where I am headed. Check the map, let's go south for a bit instead. Oh, look, there's a squiggly green-edged road, I'll see what it's like...

Again, <u>habit</u> is the key. I lost an impressive little

town for twelve years because I didn't make my notes and mark the map. I had left doing the notes for a few of days and when eventually writing them up I recalled an amazing town built on top of a huge chunk of rock in the middle of a canyon, there was one bridge across to it and otherwise the *cañón* cut deep around it. I hadn't noted the name, and though I was sure it was between Yecla in Murcia and Almeria I could not find the topography or a name that made sense on the route I thought I had taken. Doing some research for my book 'Sketches of Spain', I found it. Jorquera in the *cañón* of the Rio Júcar, north east of Albacete. I passed it the day before I thought I had.

My later memory of it was wrong in quite a few details, I should have pulled out my sketchbook right there, scribbled a little picture and made a note. OR whipped out my smart-phone and... and... did what ever you do with one.

Basic personal impressions

This is where you start putting yourself in the picture.

This example is a note made in my sketchbook as I was finishing my *café solo* after a lunch stop:

"Montorio, the *callos* was really nice, the coffee excellent, lot of road crews."

Callos is a *tapas* of intestine. At the restaurant/ bar in Montorio it was cooked with herbs and garlic and a little tomato, delicious! Elsewhere I have had it as boiled grey slugs. Montorio is just off the N-627 from Aguliar de Campoo to Burgos. The road crews and other workers go there for lunch, so it's good, and well priced.

One simple line pinned the place on my journey, the food and an observation of the people. I wish I had written more down that evening because I remember talking with a guy who admired the bike and had spotted my number plate, he came from south Wales and worked the tarmac crews in Spain.

There was a missed opportunity. But at the time I wasn't thinking of anything but the most basic details of my journey. I was up one layer and hadn't realised the potential of the layers above.

Still I did get something down, and that was the main thing.

A basic personal impression will achieve some sense of time and place, a personal reaction to a thing or event, and act as a memory key.

Although I did not write down the details of the Welshman, the mention of road crews is enough to remind me, the small bits of personal reaction being a prompt for a very important function of any journal - **The memory key.**

If you have created this key then it is often possible to add those further layers at a later date. Without it I find far too often that though I remember talking to someone in a bar, sometime during those three days, I just can't pin the memory down.

You will find me repeating this, but the smallest visual reminder can be effective.

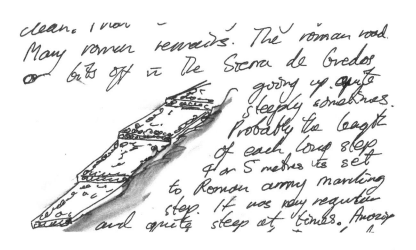

Striking a chord

This is about finding something in the experience that makes the description not only personal to you but also has a universal element that can appeal to, and strike a chord with others, even if it is in a fairly simplistic way:

"Early in the morning in the middle of France - that wonderful smell of dew-wet barley stubble; taking me back to 5.30 am cycling to summer work on a farm as a teenager."

Have you ever been out early on a country morning? One of those days that is going to be a hot one, as the day before was. The combine harvesters have been hard at work all week and the stubble fields stretch for miles. As the night's dew is lifted from the golden stalks by the rising sun it brings a unique tangy scent of straw and dust so intense it is unforgettable.

As one increases the complexity of the narrative so the use of smell and taste can be very useful in adding colour or creating a memory key for yourself and for others.

There is information more or less hidden within the paragraph above. The place and time but also information about myself. The latter is very useful as a reader will pick up on small clues like these to round their picture of the writer, without one resorting to a long-winded biography.

Striking a chord will very likely include basic personal impressions but also adds a mechanism for hooking into the reader's own memories.

As I travel I am actively looking for experiences that will spark my imagination. Something which gives me a way to put more colour into an anecdote.

Imagination is a muscle that can get weak if not exercised. In fact we all use it, all the time. It is the engine of anticipation; of, what if? It is just a matter of bringing it from subconscious to conscious use.

Flamenco á Toro Teatro.
1/04/05

Anabel with a little english to introduce to the Director of the Theatre - who knows what if anything will come of it - But Perro - una primera - A start.

More personal involvement

From that same trip through France:

"As I progress, the road signs start to sing to me and spark all sort of funny connotations it starting with a signpost to the town of Bricquebec - 'Bric-a-brac', then comes Barneville Carteret - 'Flintstones'. In my head (because my singing is appalling) I get the theme tune. Then comes St Lo - (on a roll now) - 'Sing LO, Sweet chariot', Sartilly - 'Chantilly lace', Granville - 'Open All Hours'."

I am using a very personal quirk to enliven my travel tale. I have taken the reality of passing road signs and given them my own twist, one that not that many people would have made. I have also named a number of the towns I have passed travelling down the Cherbourg peninsula, without a potentially tiresome list.

"Prudence, Déforme and Déviation, these three French beauties seem to be frequently signposted."

That old imagination is twitching away; amazing what you can do with a few road signs.

It is important that these whims get put down, sometimes it might just be a string of unconnected words. Later perhaps you can knit them into something. Here I find that sketch or notebook invaluable. It takes seconds when stopped for a drink of water or a look at the map to jot something down. That evening or at the end of the journey you can go through and type up the things worth having. Randomly typed notes in an electronic diary are more of a pain because it becomes a case of weeding out the unproductive, rather than growing the seed as one transfers it from the paper to the computer.

Personal involvement is very much apart of establishing not only your own presence in the journey but also of developing your own style of writing that hopefully, the reader will enjoy.

Imagination as reality

Imagine it is early November and months ago, you (perhaps foolishly) decided on organising a small reunion with old school friends. The idea was to take the motorbike and camp at the 'Pub With No Name' near Petersfield, which happens to be 250 miles from home. The day dawns and it is raining steadily.

I wrote about that trip titling it 'I nearly didn't do it.' It was a very wet trip.

"I am a minnow swimming against a rush of water and air. The M4 motorway, afternoon November 8th and it has been raining all day. Articulated trucks; giant salmon loom ahead and thrash up a wall of gritty water to add to that descending from the limitless grey cloud above. Behind the slight protection of my motorbike screen I wipe my goggles, the visibility does not improve and I snorkel through the truck's bow-wave at a steady 75-80 mph in the middle lane. Trout-like cars whisk by at crazy speeds and whip me with their passing wind and yet more gritty water, tainted with fuel. "

I didn't just write "a wet trip." I looked for a way of engaging the imagination of the reader in my experience, immersing them if you will.

I was so wet, and there was so much airborne water that it was like being underwater. So I made the comparison concrete, describing it as a reality.

This brings me to a word I try to avoid: 'like'. It is so easy and automatic to use when making a comparison but very easily becomes cheap and clunky or clichéd. (I even do a word search to see how many have wriggled their way into my piece).

I didn't say the trucks were <u>like</u> salmon, I said they <u>were</u> salmon. I did use trout-like. But the comparison object came first so the reader's mind would see that, before going "Oh what's it going to be like now?"

In my cake I used a number of layers from fact to fiction.

Writing a comparison as a reality gives it greater power and adds a new dimension to the account.

Damp camping at 'The Pub With No Name'

PWNN NOV 9 2013

Referencing

Here is the beginning to my 2004 Spanish adventure that took me down past Cuenca to the east of Madrid, south to Almeria and back up through Extremadura via Granada, Cordoba and the Sierra de Gredos.

"Somewhere in La Mancha, in a place whose name I do not care to remember, a gentleman...

...pulls his horse to a roadside stop, ground hitches her and slowly removes his helmet. Across the skyline march an army of enormous giants, each sedately wheeling their three arms in menacing gestures of defiance.

It is good to stop. Take a deep breath of the thick hot air of Spain, like a tasty chunk of chorizo it assaults your senses with strength and subtlety. The sharp tang of verge-heated wild herbs overlays the dust kicked up by my horse's hooves as we leave the tarmac and come to rest on the rutted dirt of the hard shoulder. Unhurriedly I remove my gloves and jacket. As I drop them across my 'Rocinante's' seat I feel a year's worth of busy-ness and stress begin to slide from me, alongside the thin trickles of sweat that start as the great August sky of Spain settles over me."

In this I have begun with a quote from Miguel

Cervantes' book 'Don Quixote', arguably the first novel written, in 1605. I continued to use it in the article as a theme thus adding a literary dimension.

If one was travelling in a jungle one might refer to Kipling's 'The Jungle Book'.

Writing style might also be 'borrowed'; one could for example, try the free form of James Joyce's 'Ulysses' to write about Ireland. If where you are seems fantastical, you could use the word patterns of 'Gullivers Travels'. A Dickensian style on the other hand might suit a crowded tenement.

Referencing a well-known part of cultural history can allow you to colour your own narrative with its overtones.

History and culture

I have read a number of travel books where I have felt that opportunities have been missed. Of course a traveller may be passing through an area in only a few days, yet I believe there is still room to avoid that feeling, that as a reader, we are in a bubble. It is a clear bubble, but one that encompasses the traveller's movements and interactions without illuminating them within the historical context of the people and place. It doesn't take much internet research these days to get a reasonable grasp of the history and culture of the countries one passes through. It doesn't need to become too detailed or exhaustive. The fact that it may well be useful in one's interactions with the locals is a side benefit.

"*Dia cinco*. Today was the ride of the whole trip. Exhausting, exhilarating, seemingly endless. Somehow the day seemed to stretch itself as I rode, to encompass the distance covered. A distance not only measured in the turns of my wheels but also in both history and geography. A journey from the Moorish, 'African' landscape of the Almeria desert, beating north and west against the receding tide of the Moorish conquest and ending in the mist-soaked Sierra de Gredos, through which the God-armed Christian knights imposed the *Reconquista*."

Spain has a very proud but complicated heritage and it imbues the culture and character of the country. It was a major part of the Roman empire but perhaps the most important factor was the 400 years of Moorish dominance. Despite a lot of talk of the purity of the modern Spaniard they have culturally and ethnically grown from a soil fertilised by their Roman, Visigothic, Moslem and Christian history.

I have been lucky enough to be the recipient of "*mi casa su casa*". This very open and honest invitation of 'my house, your house' is characteristic of the generosity that I have come across so often. Surely, a legacy of the Arab tradition of hospitality to strangers.

Without being pedantic, a little historical information can add a dab of bright colour to your account.

Landscape and character

Two fiction writers who use landscape with great effectiveness are Zane Grey and Louis L'Amour, both western writers. In many stories the landscape functions almost as an extra character. Louis L'Amour in particular is a master at describing a trail, partly because he has been down that trail himself. His stories are very often ones of travel and discovery. A lot can be learnt from the stories, not just in ways to bring scenery alive. Some of his books are written in the first person, and the techniques he uses to portray what the storyteller looks like and thinks without sounding hackneyed or obtrusive, are instructive. Louis himself was self-taught; as he drifted across the West and around the world he read anything that came his way, and with an open mind would look for knowledge, and for the craft of writing.

I think his quote "Too often I would hear men boast of the miles covered that day, rarely of what they had seen," is a very good pointer for a writing traveller. Even if you concertina the day's travel, it is the impressions that you want to pass on, not just the route and mileage. A short description of a simple moment or view, can enliven the tale of the journey.

"A symphony is playing. The silky, satin rustle of the *hojas de chopo* - poplar leaves that crowd over the little river across the road, their subtle playing fades and rises as a small breeze

conducts. The water falling from the pipe is a tympani and the string section is headed up by the cicadas that rasp and fiddle in the afternoon heat. The breeze-conductor sometimes holds up his baton and they all stop instantly for a few breaths, and perhaps the hardy little leaves of the oak trees get a chance to perform or from the river bottom comes a burst of liquid bird song."

It is important to not only <u>see</u> but also to find a way to <u>own</u> the description, make it reflect your viewpoint.

"The sharpness and extent of his nose seemed a likely handle for tipping out his drunken ramblings upon the sunflower-husked floor."

Including the wishful with the descriptive, personalises the reaction or viewpoint of the storyteller.

This can be extended even further. In the following passage from Zane Grey's 'Desert Gold' the protagonist feels the landscape is speaking to him:

"... the immensity of the star-studded sky, the soaring moon, the bleak, mysterious mountains, and limitless slope, and plain, and ridge, and valley. These things in all their magnificence had not been unnoticed by him before; only now they spoke a different meaning. A voice that he had never heard called him to see, to feel the vast hard externals of heaven and earth, all that represented the open, the free, silence and solitude and space."

An almost philosophical shading has been thrown over not only the central character but also the landscape itself.

Using a reference point beyond your own can make a simple piece of description come alive.

W. H. Hudson's 'The Purple Land', is largely an autobiographical novel about his time in South America, but also an adventure story that stands on its own. In this little extract his delicacy of touch connects the landscape he is in with the locals and with time is masterful.

"It looked like the home of a simple-minded pastoral people that had for their only world the grassy wilderness, watered by many clear streams, bounded ever by that far-off unbroken

ring of the horizon, and arched over with blue heaven, starry by night and filled by day with sweet sunshine."

Even in the simple description of landscape, pace matters; the speed at which you take the reader through your journey and at which events are described. Being aware of, and using pace to vary the reading experience is very important.

Think of it as the beating of a drum, speed it up and slow it down, give it drum rolls. At its simplest, this can be done by varying the length of sentences to speed up or slow down the rhythm of reading.

In fiction outcomes or facets of the story are often known in advance, though the how and why are revealed within. A book titled 'Cairo to Cape Town' is unlikely to end within ten miles. Key parts of the story may be anticipated or threatened before they happen in order to manipulate the reader's emotions. On the other hand the sudden revelation can be very effective.

A most remarkable bit of storytelling comes in W. H. Davies' 'The Autobiography of a Super-Tramp'. He is trying to jump a train with another hobo, but his companion was slow in clearing the step of the train as it gathered speed, and when he tried to jump his foot,

"...came short of the step and I fell, and, still clinging to the handle bar, was dragged several yards before I relinquished my hold. And there I lay for several minutes, feeling a little shaken,

whilst the train passed swiftly on into the darkness.

Even then I did not know what had happened, for I attempted to stand, but found that something had happened to prevent me from doing this. Sitting down in an upright position, I then began to examine myself, and now found that the right foot was severed from the ankle."

This shattering revelation comes out of nowhere and the impact on the reader is huge, underlined by the matter-of-fact way in which he copes with this dreadful accident, it illuminates his incredible character very effectively.

One can learn a lot from the techniques used by fiction writers as there are many examples of novelists who have also written very good travel books. One of my favourites is Robert Louis Stevenson's (author of 'Treasure Island') 'Travels with a donkey in the Cevennes', he manages to imbue the simplest of travails with a self deprecating humour and has the expert, storyteller's management of narrative pace.

As a journey is as much about what you have seen and who you have met, as where you have been, recreating impressions through expressive writing is very important.

Fiction

"My horse is growing weary. I am growing weary. Long miles, fallen behind, these have taken a toll. Fingers are numbing, wrists ache and a muscle in my leg threatens to cramp. Though we still match speed to surface there is not that smooth flow, that oneness that desires yet more road to travel. It is time to find an end, juice for 'Veloz', food and bed for me. Dusk is hard upon us, trying to overtake. The nebulous, danger hour, lights look dim as yet, but already the trail and trees are blurring together in the near distance. The 'Hour of Spirits'. Lurking tractors that turn to hedgerow shadow as you prepare yourself, shadow that hides the mud on the road until you are close upon it. Walkers suddenly appear on the verge as if coagulating from the shades of dusk. The way ahead becomes less real; it could go anywhere. Half an hour ago I could catch glimpses of it in the distance, guess its route by telephone poles and the bend of hedges. In full dark you can track it by the twists and turns of oncoming lights, trace coming corners by hot brake lights; not now. The new dampness of dusk sharpens up the days smell's; before morning it will lay them down with the dew. A farmer has been cutting silage; moments later I seem to have buried my nose in the moist tilth of a new-ploughed field. That house has a wood-burner, burning sweet apple. Phew! That one has just lit coal that stings with its acridity. Ahead the road rises to a crest outlined in tones of grey. Dropping the reins as we reach the top I coast to a stop at the roadside. A low wide valley opens its arms wide. In its heart, a small town. Lights are slowly clicking on and mist rises like moonlight from the wandering course of a river. Dark closes fast about us now. I pat Veloz's tank. "A mile or two and we'll put up." Taking up the reins I clunk us into first and Veloz's heartbeat lifts again to the song of the road that turns us on down the sweeping arms to the valley bottom."

This was a short piece I wrote as a prologue to 'Back Roads of Spain'. I wanted to draw the reader in, to paint a picture of the lone motorcyclist that would almost tell a story. At the end I admitted to the fact it is fiction but by that time hopefully it will have had the desired effect.

Something of this sort could be very useful in bringing together many days of travel which individually do not have enough significant events to warrant detailing.

You might like to try writing a short story of someone rather like you, doing something similar.

Or perhaps you want to bring the background of your trip into focus, explain why you have set out on this adventurous journey in a more interesting way. Write it in the third person which can make it easier to expand on feelings and motivations in addition to giving a voice to family and friends.

It might be useful to imagine what went on with those policemen outside of your hearing, or to recount a dream that you had (either actual or imagined) which shows your deeper feelings or fears.

Though your account of your journey is of actual happenings this does not preclude the use of fictional elements to set tone or to emphasise or explore that reality.

Beyond the Word

Photos, sketches and perhaps recorded sound can be a great resource and additional material for your account.

But be a bit wary of thinking recorded material from these sources will automatically capture the adventure. With all of these things, planning and composition are essential.

In my days of travelling with a SLR film camera one would try not to waste a signal precious frame, consequently the success rate was high. Now with a digital camera it is far too easy to take loads of shots figuring you'll find the great one in there later, or a bit of 'photoshopping' will make one.

Until I reapplied the principles of 'making the shot', I found the really decent usable shots few and far between. You have to have something reasonable to work from.

A very simple trick is to always look for a framing element, as with the photo on the next page which I used for the cover of my book 'Back Roads of Spain'. It was well into the day as I rode up to a high pass in the Sierra de Guadarrama. As a result the distance was, as is common in hot weather, hazy. I needed some foreground to provide a focus that could then travel out to the hazy promise of the distant landscape giving a journey through the picture. And I caught the edges of the trees as a frame.

This was a spur of the moment shot, of a tourist in the plaza of La Mesquita in Cordoba. I thought of sketching but didn't have a lot of time. She sat down very prettily and I took the photo.

What had caught my eye was the way in which she, the fountain behind her and the cypress tree lined up, leading the eye past the orange trees and up to the church behind. There are basic principles in the art of painting that are very useful.

Particularly this one of the 'eye path', drawing the viewer into and around the whole image.

This a case where cropping the image can be very useful in further manipulating the way the focus is moved around the picture. In the second picture the church is being framed and has to a large extent become the focal starting point. To address this because I wanted the emphasis to be the human element, I cropped it even further, re-instating the girl as the first focal point.

This brings us to the question of the resolution of a digital image. For professional printing 300 dpi is seen as the standard requirement; dpi (dots per inch) or ppi (points per inch) is the digital number of coloured dots in an inch that make up the image. The photo in the Sierra was taken at 72 dpi with 1840 x 1232 points giving an image size of 25.6" x 17.1". When the image is made smaller the dpi (resolution) will rise as the density of dots increases. At the size it is now it is at an effective 301 dpi which is fine. However at the book cover size of 14.4" x 9.4" the resolution was only 125 dpi. In fact because it does not have much in the way of foreground detail I could get away with any lack of definition. A close up of a butterfly would have been a bit blurry. In the worst cases of poor resolution the dots become visible and you get pixellation.

The Cordoba photo was taken at 200 dpi and at 1176 x 777 pixels/points/dots, this giving an image size of 5.9" x 3.9". At the size printed it has a resolution of 286 dpi and the following two respectively 285 and 276 dpi, all perfectly acceptable.

If the printed image has an effective resolution a lot higher than 300 dpi it may print too densely and be over dark. You can use photoshop to reduce the dpi by basically taking some out, but re-sampling, trying to put more in to increase resolution is rarely successful.

It is well worth really considering the equipment you are going to use to ensure that it will give good enough quality. The same rules apply to video and sound recording. In the case of video sufficient frames per second are needed to ensure it is not jerky and the resolution of the image will allow viewing on a decent sized screen. With sound, the most important item is the microphone which needs to have decent sensitivity and dynamic range.

A traditional photograph printed on photographic paper or a sketch can be digitally scanned to whatever resolution you require.

Using a sketchbook as a journal has I believe, a number of advantages. My books often have a scrappy little doodles in amongst the notes I have

made. They may or may not be usable in a book but the habit of getting the book out and finding something to draw, however simple has useful repercussions. Firstly, as it is there and open I am very likely to make some notes about the day so far and where I am. Secondly, the very act of looking at the scene in order to draw it impresses it upon one's memory in a way that taking a snap does not. Thirdly, it can often bring an interaction with passers-by. They will stop and look at someone drawing, and maybe make a comment, a connection that can start a conversation. You fiddling with your smart phone won't do that.

If one has a bit longer to sketch and you want to record your environment then you also have the advantage of being able to manipulate the image. Heighten those cliffs, make them a little closer together, perhaps bring in a framing tree trunk or foreground plant,

and of course you can leave out that ugly pylon.

The human eye and brain work in a miraculous way that is very different from a camera. We scan large areas, pick out salient features and reorganise them into a mental picture. How often have you seen a great view, grabbed the camera, taken the photos and found that when displayed they somehow don't do justice to what you felt you saw?

An artist uses composition to make an image that is more than just a hand drawn photograph.

It doesn't really matter how crude it is if what it does is give you a key to a moment. 11 years ago coming into Santander there was a big cloud bank that hid the coastline, but the heads of the Cantabrians stood tall above it, the sea seemed to merge into the cloud and it gave me an enormous sense of expectation.

The first two things to sort out are what you draw with and what you draw on. As I am mostly a motorcycle traveller, space and weight are always at a premium and affect my choices.

I do have a nice sketchbook that slides into a case, this gives it more protection from being sat on, bent or watered.

The only drawback is that the paper is slightly coloured, the sketches still work but it does mean that if I want to scan them to use in a book or as a card the paper itself stands out on a white paper. It also has a slight texture which becomes more pronounced when it is scanned. Still, I have some nice sketches on it.

Sometimes textured or woven paper can add to the impression the sketch makes.

Overall though, I favour a plain white. It must not be too glossy. I have been given a 'Moleskin' classic book but the paper is not absorbent enough.

On the other hand, some watercolour papers are too absorbent and the ink 'bleeds'.

The paper also needs to be reasonably thick or the ink will go right through. In fact I often leave the back of a page with a drawing on blank as the bright light of the scanner can pick up marks on the other side.

Wire-comb bound books are nice because they will open out right out on a single page, but the wire coil can get squidged and bent when packed tight, and with some the page doesn't lie completely flat on the scanner. The best book I've got at the moment is a stitched binding that does.

Generally speaking I find a rectangular format more flexible than square; landscape for landscape and portrait for portrait.

If you find pencil your preferred medium, then your choices of paper may differ. Whether pencil or ink, the principles are much the same. I favour ink for its immediacy and easy solidity. Pencil, for me, has always been a reversible medium in that you can erase a line that went wrong, the discipline of ink is that you need to get it right or find a creative way of making up for a mistake. Soft pencil also smudges quite easily which can be used to good effect, but it will probably then need 'fixing'. This can be done with a matt hair spray if you don't have proper fixative. Make sure you spray from a reasonable distance so you don't get any areas over wet.

I do use aquarelle pencils if I decide to add some colour, they take a little bit of practice to get the best from them, using the flat of the pencil for shading that you want to be even after light washing with a wet brush. The watercolour effect can work well with ink.

The Sevilla Alcazar. A composition note; think about how much you actually want to draw, don't commit yourself to the whole front of the palace if you are not going to have time and are going to get bored doing it.

When doing quite quick sketches it is useful to find a kind of 'abbreviation' for repetitive surfaces. You don't want to be drawing every leaf and every

stone. Here, I also used my own fingerprint to add more texture.

If I don't have any colours with me, I may use a little wine or tea, perhaps a crushed berry.

The only way to get better is to keep practising.

Recorded sound can be a very rewarding addition to the material you have to work with. But as with video and stills be sure that you have enough quality for the use to which you want to put it.

At its most basic you could use a dictaphone to record your own impressions for later transcription. A 'stream of consciousness' approach would gather a lot of information but might be tiresome to edit. The microphones built into most smart phones are not going to have good enough dynamic range and quality to be used in a presentation, an audio book or as a sound track for video. They are essentially meant for speech recording dictaphone use, though the quality can sometimes be improved by making sure that compression of the recording is minimal (it is generally set quite high to save memory space), and there may be other tweaks you can make.

PCM 44.1 Khz 16 bit Stereo is a standard that you should aim for as a minimum for usable quality. You can get a decent solid state recorder with pretty good mics for £70. It will also take input from a separate mic which can be a good option as it is more flexible in positioning, and can have better wind and speech 'pop' muffling. It will also have an on-off switch that can be used to separate a recording into tracks.

You don't have to have a script, but an idea of the sorts of uses you might put your recording to is going to be useful.

Audio is commonly 'mixed-down' from more than one track. This is great because with a very simple system you can get good results. Bear in mind that even if most of a conversation is clear, one muffled voice in the background can ruin the overall effect. And it can be very difficult to edit out the low hum from a fridge unit or wind noise, which you may well not realise is being picked up at the time. The solution is to control the environment of interviews or 'voice-overs' as much as possible - a quiet hotel room or better still, a recording studio. Breaks in the dialogue will also allow for easier editing.

Out in the real world you record 'wild tracks'. These are good lengths of background, ambient sound, whether it be the wind in pine trees or the chatter of a busy tavern. In programs such as Audacity (free), Adobe Audition or Pro Tools it is pretty easy to layer (multi-track) an interview over a 'wild track', adjusting sound levels as needed before finally getting it 'mixed-down' to a single stereo sound track.

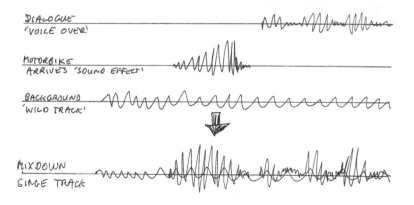

Edit and structure

When you are home again and have taken the time to put your account together it is time to be critical with it and edit - cut and embroider.

Once I am fairly happy with the result I give hard copies to anyone who is willing, or can be cajoled into reading it. I encourage them to write whatever comments they like on their copy. This feedback, whether positive or negative I have always found invaluable in polishing up the account, and seeing various viewpoints on the work.

More importantly it will trim the typos, you can read a passage you have written loads of times and still miss typos or glaring grammatical mistakes. And this will pay off if you are heading towards publication (big or small) because you will eventually need a proofreader.

Joining an online peer review group can also be well worthwhile, you review others work and get yours reviewed. Not being family or friends (who may not say exactly what they think) and potentially of an international spread is valuable. You may need to take the good with the bad though. Then come the professionals! It is well worth doing some research to find the right editorial assistance for you.

"The Society for Editors and Proofreaders (SfEP) is a professional organisation based in the UK for editors and proofreaders – the people who strive to make text accurate and readable." The SfEP promotes the highest editorial standards and offers excellent advice and information on the variety of services available and guidance on standard rates of pay. www.sfep.co.uk

For my 'Sketches of Spain' book, I chose to take on a professional editor, Jane MacNamee, who found so much during the process and made a real difference to the quality of the work. After offering me a free estimate based on the examination of an extract, she offered the work for a total of £250. It was money very well spent.

The structure of your written account is a very personal choice and is tied up with why and how you did it; so I only offer some thoughts, not a solution.

You have a cake of your ADVENTURE. You've at least half-baked it! When you are cutting it up into slices – chapters, consider not always cutting all the way down to the bottom layer.

Some experiences don't need to be defined by time and place.

Some sounds and pictures can stand on their own.

Alternatively, sometimes a passage full of facts and distances can be a good contrast and ground the narrative in the reality of the journey; how much you spent on food, fuel, accommodation, bribes or luxuries. But don't overdo it unless this is the ultimate guide book to Fragistan.

Remember, this is the STORY of an adventure.

Using the 'three act' structure of a beginning a middle and an end may seem rather obvious but it actually bears thinking about. The first section introduces the characters and motivations of the journey. The middle is where most of the action takes place and character development and change is registered. In the final part, questions are resolved, conclusions drawn and loose ends tied up, and quite possibly the scene set for the next book.

Don't automatically end a chapter at the end of the day, see if you can't end with a hook - an expectation or a danger to be tackled, something that makes the reader want to carry on reading.

Your own journey and experiences are the hardest to assess, but you will have to try and step outside of yourself and read your manuscript as a complete stranger, with a critical eye.

Good luck and *bien viaje,*

Conclusion

Through reading this book I hope you will have come to understand that YOU <u>can</u> create your own distinctive account of your adventure, whether big or small.

My sketching and my writing have been almost entirely self taught. All you need to do is make a start and give yourself some credit for being a human being with feelings and use your 'life experience' to give your unique view of the world.

The point I'm making is that however it turns out, the journal you create will be worth it just for yourself. Actually, I know that your friends and family will also appreciate it, because it has YOUR imprint upon it. To quote Matisse, "All artists' bear the imprint of their time, but the great artists are those in whom this stamp is most deeply impressed."

So, let your experience imprint, don't be shy of expressing it. After all, it is just for you... Right...

As a kid in nursery school, one thinks nothing of getting all those coloured crayons out and scribbling all over a piece of paper (and the table probably). You didn't look at what you had done and go, "Oh that's bad!" It was your expression of the moment.

Same applies now.

Bibliography

A few books which if you haven't already come across are good reads and can be learnt from.

Jupiter's Travels by Ted Simon.
Travels with a Donkey in the Cevennes by Robert Louis Stevenson.
The Tomb in Seville by Norman Lewis.
One Man Caravan by Robert E Fulton, Jnr.
The Purple Land by W. H. Hudson.
Mustang Man and Lando by Louis L'Amour.
Desert Gold by Zane Grey.
The Autobiography of a Super-Tramp by W. H. Davies.

Feel free to contact me through my websites.

www.facebook.com/DuncanRGough/
www.duncangough.wordpress.com/
www.duncangough.wixsite.com/spanish-travel